T0128782

porcupines and nightmares

by
joan cofrancesco

authorHOUSE®

AuthorHouse™
1663 Liberty Drive
Bloomington, IN 47403
www.authorhouse.com
Phone: 1-800-839-8640

Published by AuthorHouse 7/26/2012

ISBN: 978-1-4772-5248-2 (e)
ISBN: 978-1-4772-5249-9 (sc)

Thanks to the Metropolitan Art Museum for letting
me use the artwork "Porcupines" and "Nightmare" by
Robert Winthrop Chanler, 1914, for my cover.

The nightmares of my generation were AIDS and 9/11 and then there were the porcupines.

v

9/11

watching the news
at a bar in downtown manhattan
drinking miller high life
a cloud
of smoke
rolls by

my cat stretches
and yawns
then stares at me
on the bed
reading lorca
we have nowhere to go

no muse

i placed all my crap
into a puma
gym bag
and dragged my ass
to the treadmill

heated sake
by the woodstove
as evening came
and the snow continued
and we didn't care

fallen leaves along
the erie canal path
boy in red sneakers

wearing only
a silk black bathrobe
she flashes me

egyptian cobra
descendant of the asp
that killed cleo
slithers away
from the bronx zoo

lavender sky
where the
twin towers
used
to
be

staring at
chaler's
painting
porcupines + nightmare
think of you

liz just died
i'm sitting here
listening to jane's addiction
drinking merlot

1981
ronnie turns his head away
and thousands die

in the er
watching
a fly crawling
upside down
on the ceiling

panic
t-cell count
less
than
500

plague

we were all afraid
nobody knew
where it came from
sunken face
purple blotches
i never kissed you
goodbye

mr. death

with his glass cane
filled with rainbows and skulls
he glides the sidewalks
i sit at my desk
listening to birds
outside my window
i stare at him
my fingers resting
on page 24 of
milton

exhausted
watching
black crows
fly in the
haze
a lawnmower
rusting in
the
fall
rain

in this
stainless steel
world
of bedpans
and forceps
i see a
person's
flesh

HIV test –
dead blackbird
on porch

rain

your watercolor rat
hangs above
my bed

let's stay in
and watch old
bettie davis movies

high cost of love

night sweats
gaunt cheeks –
was that one night
in barcelona
worth it?

went to the whitney
dekoonings
a pollock
some warhols
but
it was the mapplethorpe
polaroids that got me
cock and balls
laid out flat
on
a wooden
slab

today 321
is a dead patient
16 get well cards
on his nightstand

your drawing
of your light blue cat
sam
keeps you alive
andy

a beautiful woman
long smooth legs
steps out
of a 2000 mazda
miata
on the edge
of a manhattan
street
and in the sky
the twin towers
come down
in flames

weak thin arms
he is hanging balloons
and disco ball
putting 1982 banner
across the wall
wondering if this is
the last time

reagan couldn't
even say the
word AIDS
till rock hudson
appeared on tv

we were reckless
wandered together
through nyc
rainbow flags
down 5th ave.
pride parades
bath houses bars
and now
yr lifeless
bedpan shining
in the sunlight

terrorist car bomb
near the lion king
at times square

christmas tree dying
christmas berries glowing
blood red
like memories

christmas
bells ring
he is come
but you are gone

my life is like
a robert frank
black and white snap
a poet
on a road
in the middle of
nowhere

in the zendo
nothing
but the smell of rain

sunday
i lie in bed
with my cat
listening to church bells
another beyond day

in the bathtub
with black candles around it
i smell the woodstove
patchouli incense
my next smoke-filled
air

ash wednesday
the twin towers
are down

warm days
cool nights
sauvignon blanc
pop art
camel cigarettes
in the afterglow

stroking my black
cat, i listen
to billie's riffs
then read
mayakovsky
and fall asleep
blue off-the-air glimmer
on my set

under the spell of rimbaud
lovemaking with you
in cemeteries
and under falls

we drove
in the east village
in your open mg
like two gurgling
draft beer spouts

sometimes i feel
like a monk
writing poems alone
in front of my fire
but i'd rather feel
like an alley cat

perfect

on this hot
august afternoon
in a lavender
bubblebath
i listen to
'trane
and read
four quartets

i remember
the marlboro man
masculine handsome

my fingers are stained
my house stinks
my white cat is grey

my dog
has your black panties
between his teeth
and they're covered
with dust

i pour myself
a glass of wine
and get too close
to the fire

i stroll along
the tow path
of the erie canal
accompanied by
a watersnake

art

the urinal
called mutt
in the center
of the museum

lovemaking
in an old venice-style
hotel
to a baroque concert
in st mark's square

poet

kaiken goose
flies back and forth
over the andes
that's all he ever does

i'd drink
expensive red
with my toast every morning
i'd look like angelina
and write like frank
i'd live in provincetown
in a loft overlooking the sea
with 10 siamese cats
who all have blue
crossed eyes

old pegasus gas sign
is slowly becoming
a poem

for 70 years

full moon fills
the room

on a chair
in front of the yankees game
my father snores

in my black ny baseball cap
painting my apartment
to vivaldi
brushing to the violin
white paint flying
onto blue jeans and black cats
zen master
lost in the strokes

gruyere de comte

the montbeliard cow
is the only cow

frank o'hara
boris butts
and now ai
all gone

i doze
towns burn
along the mak cong

i wake to walter
saying
goodnight

the poet

in a black turtleneck
and beret
the holy ghost says
to me
didn't give you
much of a choice
did we kid

portia

racy red
curvy soul
filled with
chrome

van gogh's shoes
rivers' camels
twin towers crumbling
dekooning's yellow slash
your naked thighs
always

candle incense desire
to touch
your thigh
and you letting me
for first time

especially
the way you
rub up against me
like a roaming pussy
is it love
or are you just
marking your territory

at the monastery
i see monks
and
shinto cows

walking home from school
chestnuts
in my front pocket

last night
i dreamt
i was naked and howling
with allen & jack
in the village

in your A frame
on oversized persian pillows
in ripped jeans
encircled by
pollacks and dekoonings
rumi
in your head

it felt like
we were still skiing
hot rum toddies
in front
of our fireplace

poem to barry gifford

evening, syracuse –
   woman in window
leaning on the ridge, inhaling
      a joint
   she remembers
        janis joplin
   3 flights up
heavy, high
   exhaling pain
into
   the summer night

hot august night
blue 'trane
so soft in the night
as i write
the same poem
over
and
over
and
over
again

the roaches
can't eat poetry
so they wander
next door
where the
chinese live

when the grammar is proper
when the jewelry is sparkly
when the tools have power
the october day has 90 degrees
and the algebra is linear
and easy

to ignore the world
and after a feast
of filet mignon
and cabernet sauvignon
fuck all night long

greek peak

i feel like
ulysses
skiing down
elysian fields
while you
wait like
penelope
in the lodge
with hot
rum cider
by the
fire

in bed
reading zen
by a fading
candle

the ones with
the jealous gods
say that
being promiscuous
we deserve it
white spider
on your yankees cap

ice freezes
on my curls
when will i get home

your lips red
from wine
i feel like verlaine

i live alone
in a
studio apartment
and read
nothing
but
bukowski
i sleep
alone
and
dream
of
walking
down
wall street
at
rush
hour

i dawdle
on white crisp sheets
windchimes

last night
i had a dream
that a woman
was putting
a green cover
over a x-mas tree
it had an eye
in the middle
of it
like the one
on the dollar
bill

rolling waves
hit the sand
no thoughts of tomorrow

it's normal

i love to sleep
in a cottage
in provincetown
and
hear the rain
pounding the roof
and the gay
guys next
door
banging
away
to
club
music
and then
waking up
with
you and
collect
shells
and
stones
along
the beach

we tap the dragons
on the sides of our purple goblets
together
in an unmade bed
fog will be here
by morning
he waits tables
at a café
in soho
crosses the hudson
each evening
climbs to his small
room in brooklyn
and writes poems
into the midnight

dracula movie
at the commercial
taking a piss

ultrasound
green cold
jelly
across my teeth—
what's eating me!

21
looking out
the window of sam's apartment
summer of love
wandered down to
washington square park
then to times square
the guys went to
the bathhouses
i went to
gotham book mart

wandering through soho
in your
calvin klein black
tight jeans
and bomber leather jacket
and scarf
how devastating
you looked

nyc
1981
drank like piaf
loved like anais nin
i romanticized nyc
like isherwood
did berlin
it was
disco
art
stonewall
gays
then
AIDS

the kiss of death (love can kill you)

poppers
bathhouses
grace jones
all it took was one
glance
one nod
who would have guessed?

you were once as happy
as a bottle of wine
with a 1913 vintage
then in came
the man with the scythe